BRITISH RAILWAYS IN TRANSITION

THE CORPORATE BLUE AND GREY PERIOD 1964–1997

BRITISH RAILWAYS IN TRANSITION

THE CORPORATE BLUE AND GREY PERIOD 1964–1997

Jim Blake

PEN & SWORD
TRANSPORT

AN IMPRINT OF PEN & SWORD BOOKS LTD.
YORKSHIRE – PHILADELPHIA

First published in Great Britain in 2018 by
Pen & Sword Transport
An imprint of
Pen & Sword Books Ltd
Yorkshire - Philadelphia

ISBN 9781526703163

Typeset in Aura Technology and Software Services, India
Printed and bound in India, by Replika Press Pvt. Ltd.

Pen & Sword Books Ltd incorporates the Imprints of Pen & Sword Books Archaeology, Atlas, Aviation, Battleground, Discovery, Family History, History, Maritime, Military, Naval, Politics, Railways, Select, Transport, True Crime, Fiction, Frontline Books, Leo Cooper, Praetorian Press, Seaforth Publishing, Wharncliffe and White Owl.

For a complete list of Pen & Sword titles please contact

PEN & SWORD BOOKS LIMITED
47 Church Street, Barnsley, South Yorkshire, S70 2AS, England
E-mail: enquiries@pen-and-sword.co.uk
Website: www.pen-and-sword.co.uk

or
PEN AND SWORD BOOKS
1950 Lawrence Rd, Havertown, PA 19083, USA
E-mail: Uspen-and-sword@casematepublishers.com
Website: www.penandswordbooks.com

Cover Photo: Pressed Steel single unit L125 (motor brake second 55025) is one of two seen at Acton Main Line Station on 14 October 1989 working a 'Thames Trains' through service from Paddington to Greenford via Ealing Broadway.

Cover Photo: At Clapham Junction in April 1990, a good variety of rolling stock may be seen, ranging from an English Electric Class 50 Co-Co diesel to a Class 73 electro-diesel Bo-Bo and various types of Southern Region EMUs.

For Rear Cover: One of the seemingly everlasting Western Region Class 253 HST's speeds through Reading Station in October 1996.

Introduction

This photographic survey looks at a variety of British Rail diesel and electric locomotives and multiple units, from the mid-1960s to the time of BR's full privatisation in 1997. The thirty or so years involved encompass the deliveries of the last of what now are referred to as 'first generation' diesel and electric rolling stock, to the appearance of many types of modern traction that are still in service today.

In many respects, diesels and electrics were somewhat neglected by photographers in the mid and late 1960s, when British Rail's last steam locomotives were being withdrawn from service and, to some extent, for a few years afterwards. This certainly applied to my own photographic output, though as the pictures in this book will show, I *did* photograph types that even in those days were becoming extinct. It was the withdrawal of older electric multiple units (notably on the Southern Region) and types of diesel locomotive that were considered non-standard from the late 1960s onwards that prompted more general interest in 'modern traction' and in any case, since steam had ended in August 1968, it was a natural progression anyway.

By the early 1970s, several of the first generation diesel locomotives were being withdrawn from service. These ranged from the ill-fated 'baby Deltics' which worked suburban services on my local Great Northern lines, to the Western Region's large fleet of diesel hydraulics, which much to the consternation of Swindon management, were deemed non-standard by the BR hierarchy and therefore slated for early withdrawal and replacement by their favoured diesel electrics.

The time period covered by the photographs in this book also reflects the break-up and eventual privatisation of British Rail, which may be clearly seen by a gradual change from the corporate BR 'rail blue' livery first seen in 1964 to various regional liveries and route-branding, most notably Network SouthEast whose services stretched all the way from East Anglia to Exeter.

In the time covered by this book, I travelled quite a lot around the country mainly to film and photograph buses and trolleybuses (as well, of course, as BR steam until its final demise) but, fortunately, also captured on film diesel and electric rolling stock at places as diverse as Perth, Cardiff, Manchester, Ely, Portsmouth and Rye. From 1987 onwards, owing to the demise of 'slam-door' diesel and electric multiple units, I also travelled extensively around the Network SouthEast area specifically to photograph them, which will explain why there is a greater proportion of pictures of such stock in this book. However, I was also able to capture on film a good variety of 'first generation' diesel locomotives on both freight and passenger workings during this period as well as some of the newer locos then replacing them. Seeing some of the latter in BR livery was of course to be a short-lived spectacle.

Most of the photographs included herein have not been published before, and I hope that readers will find them of interest. Grateful thanks go to Colin Clarke who has spent about six years scanning my 100,000-strong collection of negatives, to my editor John Scott-Morgan, and also to Ken Wright for his help in ironing out a number of queries that arose whilst compiling this book.

Jim Blake,
Palmers Green,
September 2018

How the mighty have fallen! One of the two pioneer LMS/English Electric main line diesel locomotives, 10001, shunts wagons across the Grand Union Canal near Old Oak Common MPD on 31 December 1964. By now, it was the only survivor of the pair, and was finally withdrawn early in 1966.

From the beginning of January 1967, the famous Bournemouth Belle Pullman was scheduled to be worked by Brush 4 (Class 47) diesels loaned from the Western Region, though right up to the end of steam six months later, steam locomotives often hauled it instead. On Saturday 3 June 1967, however, a serious shortage of serviceable locos has led BRCW/Crompton type 3 Bo-Bo D6527 to be used for the down Belle. It is seen here south of Woking.

On 8 October 1967, North British diesel hydraulic type 2 B-B D6328 looks smart in current BR rail blue livery when seen on empty stock working at Paddington. By now, however, the writing was on the wall for this class of fifty-eight locomotives, all of which were withdrawn by the early 1970s.

Pre-war Southern Railway EMUs were still very much in service in 1968. Outside Brighton Station on 8 June that year, 2BIL unit 2096 is stabled. These were introduced in 1935, remaining in service until 1971, when replaced by such types as the 4VEP.

During 1957/58, three classes of type 1 Diesel were introduced by British Railways for use on pick-up goods services, particularly on local branches. The first were the English Electric locos starting with D8000, which were to become very numerous and later be designated Class 20. Next there was a batch of fifty British Thompson-Houston built type 1s, numbered from D8200 onwards, and then ten North British-built locos, numbered from D8400. The latter two types were all allocated to the Eastern Region, many in the London area, but the NBL engines were all withdrawn by the end of 1968, followed by the BTH examples. In the latter case, closure of branch lines and also goods yards at local stations, rendered the class redundant by 1971. Thus, D8233 of this type is one of the last survivors when seen at Finsbury Park Diesel Depot on 3 June 1969. However, it became static train electric heating unit DB968000 after withdrawal, lasting for ten years or so in this capacity and surviving to be preserved. It is presently at the East Lancashire Railway. Also of note in this picture is the new block of flats being built in the background. This is one of four pre-fabricated 'Bison' tower blocks built for the GLC's Harvist Estate, and some of the last such blocks built in London. Whereas others have long-since been demolished, these were inherited by Islington Council who spent several million pounds refurbishing them in 1999/2000.

At Finsbury Park diesel depot the same day, four English Electric type 2 Bo-Bo 'Baby Deltics' D5903, D5908, D5904 and D5900 forlornly await their fate. Built only in 1959, this ten-strong class, used on Great Northern suburban services, had always been troublesome, most being 'grounded' as early as 1964. Formal withdrawals began in the autumn of 1968 and only two survived into the 1970s. These four were scrapped shortly after this picture was taken.

By 9 May 1970, express passenger services on the Woodhead Tunnel route between Manchester and Sheffield had been withdrawn, but freight services remained. Here, 1.5kv BR Doncaster-built Class EM1 Bo-Bo 26027 double-heads a westbound freight through Dinting Station.

On the same day, a group of class EM1 and EM2 Bo-Bos are seen outside their Reddish Depot. The Woodhead route finally closed in 1981, to the outrage of many people considering that it had only been electrified in 1954! To this day, plans are afoot to reopen it.

This is all that remains of BR 204hp 0-6-0 diesel shunter D2140 outside Swindon Works on 12 April 1971. It had been built there in April 1960 and withdrawn ten years later, after service at Taunton and Laira MPDs.

Seen on the same day, D601 *Ark Royal* was the second of five type 4 diesel hydraulics of the Warship class built by North British for the Western Region in 1958. These locos were very troublesome, therefore all had been withdrawn by the end of 1967. The first two were sold for scrap to Woodham Brothers of Barry, where this one is seen, whereas the other three went to Cashmore's at Newport. The latter were quickly broken up, but along with the two hundred or so steam engines languishing at Barry, D600 and D601 were not. D600 was scrapped in 1970, yet D601 survived in Woodham's yard until 1980, apparently since there were plans afoot to save it. But it was not to be and, like its namesake during the Second World War, *Ark Royal* was sunk without trace.

On 15 June 1972, a three-car London Midland Region Class 501 unit has just crossed the first of two level crossings in Bollo Lane, Acton, on the North London Line's Broad Street to Richmond service. As may be seen, these units were still using fourth-rail electrification at the time, though subsequently this was changed to third-rail.

Although the Western Region's early diesel locomotives, such as the Warships, were diesel hydraulics, the Bristol Pullman sets introduced in 1960 were diesel electrics, with North British/M.A.N. engines and Metropolitan Cammell bodywork. On 17 April 1973, driving motor car W60096 awaits departure from Paddington's platform 6 in the evening rush hour not long before these units were withdrawn.

Shortly before their withdrawal, driving motor car W60092 is at the trailing end of the South Wales Pullman's evening departure from Paddington on 27 April 1973. As may be seen, I am not the only photographer present that evening, although the days when this platform was thronged with railway enthusiasts, which I remember in the late 1950s and early 1960s, are already long gone.

On 10 July 1973, a Class 47 Brush 4 Co-Co heads an up express on the Great Northern main line past the former Standard Telephone & Cable Works factory at New Southgate. Soon, overhead catenary will mar this view from Oakleigh Road when the Great Northern suburban electrification scheme is under way.

On 28 July 1973 an early BR Derby-built DMU loads up at the new Stevenage Station on a stopping service to Kings Cross. The station has only recently been opened and is directly adjacent to the main shopping centre and bus station of Stevenage New Town, which had been developed in the early post-war years. I had relatives move there from London in the mid-1950s, and visiting them entailed travelling by train to the original Stevenage Station, at the northern end of the 'old town' which itself was some distance to the north of the New Town Centre, and then a lengthy bus ride. How inane that it took more than 25 years to relocate the station to be convenient for the growing New Town!

By 16 March 1974, only the Westerns remained of the diesel hydraulics that had once dominated the Western Region main lines to South Wales and the West Country. D1031 *Western Rifleman* accompanies a Class 47 (which type in many cases replaced the Westerns) at Swindon. Withdrawal of the class had already begun by now; this one perished in February 1975.

Fellow Western 1035 *Western Yeoman* changes crew at Cardiff General Station on 15 April 1974 before heading further west. This one was withdrawn in January 1975.

On 18 August 1976, its first day in service, brand new EMU 313017 arrives at Drayton Park Station to run the short distance through the former Great Northern & City Railway tube tunnels to Old Street. Trains only ran thus in passenger service until the full Great Northern inner suburban electric service between Moorgate and Hertford North or Welwyn Garden City began on 8 November. The EMU is using ramps built in 1939 to connect this isolated tube line with the LNER branches to Highgate, Alexandra Palace, High Barnet and Edgware at Finsbury Park, thereby linking it (at East Finchley) with the main Northern Line. Work had to be stopped during the Second World War and was finally abandoned in the early 1950s – comprising the now-infamous uncompleted Northern Line extensions. Thus, the link from Drayton Park to the main line, meant to have opened in 1940, finally became operative in 1976! As this book is being compiled in the spring of 2016, the original Class 313 EMUs used on this service, which operate as 25kv overhead north of Drayton Park, but on a 630dc third rail in the tunnel section to Moorgate, still serve the line.

A type of London Underground train which served the Northern City Line between 1939 and 1966, still survived in service at this period on the Isle of Wight – the 1923-35 LT Standard Stock which had also worked on the Central, Piccadilly and main Northern Lines. On 6 September 1976, three-car 3VEC unit No.032 (to give it its Southern Region terminology) is coupled with a four-car 4TIS unit when seen heading south between Brading and Sandown. Redundant tube stock such as this was used to replace steam on the Island's surviving Ryde to Shanklin line (in early 1967) owing to very restricted clearances in the tunnel between Ryde St. John's Road and Esplanade Stations. The elderly tube cars survived until 1989/90, only to be replaced by newer ones built in 1938. Some of these are still in use at the time of writing, though trains are only in two-car formations now – not seven as seen here.

Needed for shunting on the Island line, Hunslet 204hp 0-6-0 diesel shunter 05001 was new in 1956 as 11140, later renumbered D2554. It came to the island in June 1966 and was no doubt much in demand while the line was being electrified. It is seen at Shanklin on 6 September 1976. Withdrawn in 1981, it has subsequently been preserved.

Seen at a snowy Chadwell Heath Station on New Year's Day 1979, Eastern Region three-car EMU 052 heads for Shenfield, and will soon be replaced by new Class 315 sets. Given the nickname 'Shenfield Sliders', these units were the first main line EMU's in the London area to have sliding doors, and originated from the 1935-40 New Works Programme to improve commuter services in London. The war delayed their introduction until 1949.

On 14 May 1979, passenger services were restored along part of the eastern section of the former North London Railway from where they had been withdrawn as a result of bomb damage during the Second World War. Curiously, though, at first they ran non-stop between Stratford (Low Level) and Canonbury, where motor brake second car E50366 leads a two-car Cravens DMU on the first day. The new service initially ran from North Woolwich to Stratford, including a new station providing interchange with the District Line at West Ham, then non-stop to Canonbury and along the existing North London Line as far as Camden Road. 'New' stations along the previously closed section were eventually provided at Dalston Kingsland, Hackney Central, Homerton and Hackney Wick, basically on the sites of the long-closed originals.

On the same day, BRCW driving trailer composite E56188 is seen at Canning Town Station at the trailing end of a Tottenham Hale to North Woolwich train, which had shared the same tracks as the new service to and from Camden Road since Stratford. The station here, north of the A13, is being reconstructed, yet would be closed in the late 1990s and resited the other side of the bridge. Today it forms an interchange with the Jubilee Line and two branches of the Docklands Light Railway, one of which took over the branch to Stratford in 2011, whilst meanwhile the line to North Woolwich had been closed in 2006, effectively replaced by another new DLR branch to Woolwich Arsenal.

The mainstay of North London Line services, and those from Euston to Watford, at this time was still the L.M.R. Ashford-built class 501 EMUs, dating from the mid-1950s. Motor open brake second car M61175 leads one of these into Camden Road Station on 16 May 1979. By now, these units had been converted to operate on third-rail electrification.

Two English Electric type 1 Bo-Bos, 20213 & 20056, are seen hauling a coal train on the Manchester to Sheffield Woodhead route at Wombwell on 5 July 1979. This view was taken from the scrapyard of Wombwell Diesels, who broke up thousands of London Transport RT, RTL, RTW and RF-class buses in the 1960s and 1970s.

Illustrating what may be seen as the beginnings of the break-up of British Rail, Metro-Cammell driving trailer composite car E56377 bears 'Regional Railways' grey and blue livery when seen calling at Huntingdon with a stopping train from Peterborough to Hitchin on 10 July 1979.

At Peterborough itself, English Electric Type 3 Co-Co 37054, based at March, calls with a semi-fast service, the 10.05 from Kings Cross on which I had travelled there. This type had made its debut at Stratford MPD early in 1961, and some examples are still in service today.

BR Sulzer type 2 Bo-Bos 25038 & 25153 double-head a cross-country service, also at Peterborough on 10 July 1979. Although contemporary to the class 37s, all of these had been withdrawn from service by early 1987.

On the Midland Main Line, B.R/Sulzer type 4 1Co-Co1 'Peak' 45001 (originally D13) heads an up semi-fast service comprising only four carriages at West Hampstead on 31 August 1979. This class too became extinct during the 1980s. The view of this main line too will soon be marred by overhead catenary, in this case for the electrification of local services between Bedford and Moorgate.

In the suburban side of Kings Cross Station, on platform ten, EMU 313028 heads a six-car formation bound for Hertford North that for some reason has been diverted here from Moorgate on Friday, 14 September 1979. During the 1980s, weekend services to Moorgate were withdrawn, along with those on late evenings during the week, meaning Class 313's could be seen at Kings Cross at those times. However, all-day, all-week services to Moorgate, using the same units, were restored in December 2015.

On the same day, Deltic 55011 *The Royal Northumberland Fusiliers* arrives at Kings Cross platform seven to haul the 1805 departure to York. By now, these locomotives had been ousted from their top-link duties on the East Coast Main Line by HST sets, and all were withdrawn by early January 1982. Note the board on the right, complete with London Transport 'bullseye' for the working site for the link between Kings Cross Midland (i.e. Metropolitan Widened Lines) Station and the Piccadilly and Victoria Line Underground stations – it is on the site of the former York Way Station, and materials for the scheme were carted along the disused tunnels leading between the two.

Other preparation works in connection with the 'Kings Cross Midland' project may be seen here at Radlett on 16 September 1979 in the form of masts for the overhead catenary needed for the new EMU's that will work between Bedford and Moorgate, via the Widened Lines. BR Derby motor brake second M51627, part of the fleet of four-car DMUs that had replaced steam on these services in the early 1960s and which will itself be replaced by the new EMUs, heads an up stopping service to St. Pancras.

Some overhead gantries are in place, too, as BR Sulzer type 4 1Co-Co1 Peak 45141 heads a down express through Radlett on the same occasion.

Two of the diesel locomotive types that could be seen at Kings Cross in the early 1960s are seen here on 13 April 1980, in the shape of English Electric type 4 1Co-Co1 40028 (originally D228 and once named *Samaria*) and a Brush 2 Class 31 A1A-A1A. By now, Class 40s were being withdrawn and were no longer seen here very often.

Workmen putting the finishing touches to the 'new' Hackney Central Station take a tea break in the sun on 12 May 1980 as a two-car DMU on the Camden Road to North Woolwich service passes through, with BR Derby motor brake second car E50845 at its trailing end. The station opened a few days later, but was not really 'new' at all, being on the site of the North London Railway Hackney station that had closed in 1944. Its original entrance may be seen above the DMU and still exists today, in use as a 'trendy' wine bar.

On 25 May 1980, Brush 4 Co-Co 47425 arrives at Wood Green Great Northern Station with the 0634 special to Manchester Victoria for spectators attending the 150th anniversary celebrations of the Rainhill Trials. Somewhat curiously, it travelled via the Hertford Loop.

Upon arrival at Manchester Victoria, I was able to catch this view of BR/Sulzer type 2 Bo-Bo 25270, which appears to be on station pilot duties. As mentioned earlier, the writing was now on the wall for this class.

Spectators, including myself, were taken to Rainhill on DMUs such as that led by BR Derby motor brake second M51672, seen here after arrival.

At an open day at Stratford MPD and Works on 11 July 1981, one of the guest exhibits is Southern Region BRCW type 3 Bo-Bo 33056 *The Burma Star*, which accompanies an electro-diesel of Class 73.

Nicely repainted in a distinctive variation of BR livery, complete with large fleet number leaving no doubt about its identity, Brush 4 Co-Co 47583 *County of Hertfordshire* is one of Stratford's own allocation, and typifies the Class 47s that hauled expresses on the Great Eastern main line prior to electrification. It was allocated there from 1975 until withdrawal in 2004.

English Electric type 3 Co-Co 37265 is typical of the many locomotives of this class that were shedded at Stratford for many years, from when they were first introduced early in 1961. It too was based there for much of its working life, from 1969 until withdrawal in 2000.

Deltic 55016 *Gordon Highlander* heads a railtour off the Lea Valley line to the Tottenham & Hampstead line when seen passing Downhills Park, Tottenham on 28 November 1981. All surviving Deltics would be withdrawn six weeks later; this one was preserved. Behind it is the awful new GLC Ferry Lane Estate, nicknamed 'The Rabbit Hutches' by locals at the time.

On the same day, one of the 25kv electric locomotives new for the West Coast Main Line Electrification is seen at Cricklewood MPD in the guise of ADB968021. This was formerly No.84003, and used as a load bank testing locomotive. Originally, it was numbered E3038, one of six Bo-Bos supplied by North British to a GEC design in 1960.

Also at Cricklewood, two former LMR Class 501 EMU driving motors have been converted to battery locomotives for use in conjunction with electrification work on what was then referred to as the Midland City Line, and renumbered as cars 97704 and 97705. Their roofs have been cut down to ensure safe passage through the Metropolitan Widened Lines tunnels between Kentish Town and Moorgate. At this period, the introduction of new EMUs on this service was delayed owing to a protracted industrial dispute: the new trains finally ran in the summer of 1983. Some of these battery locomotives survive today, being needed especially for engineers' trains on the Finsbury Park to Moorgate line.

BR/Sulzer Type 2 Bo-Bo 25173 is seen on 1 September 1982 running light engine near Harlesden Station on the West Coast Main Line, when based at Cricklewood. More than 300 of this type were built in the 1960s, though by now they were rapidly being withdrawn. This one however has been preserved.

The Hertford Loop is frequently used to divert trains from the Great Northern (East Coast) Main Line when engineering works require possession of it, particularly on the twin-track bottleneck in the Welwyn area. On 28 November 1982, an HST set speeds north through my local station, Palmers Green. Quite often, such diversions necessitate the reduction or even suspension of my local train service, particularly on Sundays!

BR/Sulzer Peak type 4 1Co-Co1 46010 is seen undergoing attention in Stratford Works on 9 July 1983. Somewhat oddly, it was withdrawn only just over a year later, but was subsequently preserved.

Electric services between Moorgate (Met) and Bedford have finally begun operating after a long-running industrial dispute as new EMU 317307 arrives at Barbican Station on 11 July 1983, working a stopping service to Luton. Less than five years later, most services from Bedford and Luton were diverted at Farringdon to run to such destinations as Brighton or Sutton upon the reopening of Snow Hill Tunnel and the introduction of Thameslink services, using new Class 319 EMUs instead. The small remnant of services from the Midland lines to Moorgate was finally withdrawn in the spring of 2009, since works for enlarging Farringdon Station for Thameslink's upgrade fouled the tracks that led to Moorgate on the former Metropolitan Widened Lines, necessitating their removal. Class 317 units were redeployed to replace slam-door stock such as Class 312's on the former Eastern Region.

Representing older stock working local services in the London Area, Cravens motor brake second E53360 heads a train of two two-car units at Tidal Basin on 29 August 1983. It has come from North Woolwich and is working only as far as Stratford. The scenery in this area has changed dramatically since this picture was taken, not least with the opening of new Docklands Light Railway branches, and the closure of this railway line between Stratford and North Woolwich at the end of 2006. Part of it, however, will be reused for Crossrail when that opens in 2018.

Former Woodhead route Class EM1 Bo-Bo 76004 makes a sad sight heading a line of its fellows at C.F. Booth's Rotherham scrapyard on 7 January 1984. Condemned BR Standard Mk1 carriages complete the picture.

London, Tilbury & Southend Line EMU 308 314, which has recently been refurbished, heads a formation of two of these units at Purfleet Station with an up train to Fenchurch Street on 4 April 1984. When new, this class of EMUs included baggage cars for services that connected with ocean liners at Tilbury Docks.

On 1 June 1984, two English Electric type 3 Co-Cos, 37021 and 37103, head a container freight off the North London Line en route for the West Coast Main Line when seen passing Willesden Junction Low Level Station. They will probably be replaced by an electric locomotive a little further on in the sidings at Stonebridge Park. Today, the route through to either Stratford or Tilbury has been electrified throughout, obviating such a change.

Captured from the window of a Charing Cross to Hastings express on 27 August 1984, rows of withdrawn ex-Southern Railway 4SUB EMUs make a sad sight at Grove Park, especially as some have been set on fire, presumably by vandals. Others have had their windows smashed by such mindless morons. The last of this type had been withdrawn from service in the spring of 1983.

On the same day, Hastings six-car unit No.1017 is one of a twelve-car formation that has carried me to Hastings for a day out. These Eastleigh-built units were built in 1956/57 to a special narrow width to negotiate the restricted loading gauge, particularly in tunnels, on this main line. Their driving motor cars were also peculiar to the Southern Region in having their engine compartments behind the drivers' cabs; travelling in the passenger compartment in the trailing end of these was therefore a very lively experience. This led to their being nicknamed 'Thumpers'. They were withdrawn upon electrification of the main line in 1986 (achieved by singling the track through restricted tunnels), but one unit has been preserved and is still active today.

Another Southern region oddity is driving motor brake second S13004S of unit 4902, one of two Bulleid-designed double-deck four-car (4DD) sets built in 1949. Owing to the awkwardness of their seating configuration which increased dwell times at stations, the type was not perpetuated but they remained in service, usually running between Charing Cross and Dartford, until 1971/72. On 19 October 1984, this one has turned up in sidings in London's Docklands at Silvertown. It is one of two saved for preservation, on which gradual restoration work is ongoing.

Nicely painted in current BR blue and grey livery, BR Derby motor second car 53921 heads a three-car formation towards North Woolwich on 19 November 1984. As may be seen, this line has now been reduced to single-track, but as evident by the conductor rail visible on the right, will be converted to third-rail EMU operation in May 1985.

On the same day, a little nearer to North Woolwich terminus, Brush type 2 A1A-A1A 31223 is at the rear of a formation headed by Gresley's A3 Pacific 4472 *Flying Scotsman* which has graced this backwater by attending the ceremonial opening of North Woolwich Station Museum, at which HRH Queen Elizabeth, The Queen Mother, officiated. The museum, which was administered by Newham Council, housed small exhibits in the original station buildings as well as various rolling stock in adjacent sidings. However, the latter was often vandalised and the whole project eventually starved of funds – the museum closed in 2008.

Representing what was then hoped to be British Rail's future, Advanced Passenger Train APT-P speeds past Kensal Green Station heading north on the West Coast Main Line on 12 April 1985. Alas, thanks to Margaret Thatcher's disdain for public transport, the project was scrapped not long after this picture was taken, however lessons learned in the operations of the prototypes were put to good use in the construction of later rolling stock, not least the Class 91 electric locomotives on the East Coast Main Line.

This scene at Broad Street shows two of the North London Line's own Class 501 units, and Bulleid-designed Southern Region 2EPB set No. 6321 on 17 April 1985. A month later, the latter type would replace 501s on North London Line services from Richmond, which were diverted from Canonbury to run via Dalston Kingsland and Stratford to North Woolwich instead, replacing the DMU service that had been introduced in 1979. The dilapidated Broad Street terminus, which had never been fully repaired after wartime bomb damage, would henceforth see only a handful of trains to and from Watford Junction in rush hours, before final closure in June 1986. The replacement of three-car EMUs by older two-car ones on the North London Line fully epitomises the government of the day's loathsome attitude towards public transport, and public service in general!

At Dalston Western Junction, English Electric type 3 Co-Co 37050 heads a freight composed of oil tankers eastwards on 8 May 1985. The tracks on the left are to and from Dalston Junction Station and Broad Street; those on the right head towards Stratford and the east.

Looking from the same bridge in the other direction, two Cravens two-car DMUs pass on the Camden Road-Stratford-North Woolwich service in Dalston Kingsland Station. Ironically, this station had been opened in 1850, but closed in 1865 when nearby Dalston Junction opened. It was rebuilt and reopened in May 1983, for the services seen here, and a few days after this picture was taken, two-car ex-Southern region 2EPB EMUs replaced these DMUs, running from Richmond to North Woolwich.

To mark the electrification of the North Woolwich branch, and the retirement of Class 501 units from the main North London Line, unit 501 150 is seen coupled to one of its fellows working an LCGB railtour over the North London and Euston-Watford lines on 11 May 1985. It has just been to North Woolwich, where Class 501s never operated in service, when seen heading north through Silvertown Station. Electric services using Southern Region 2EPB units began along this section of line the following day.

Brush 2 A1A-A1A 31201 passes through Lea Bridge Station on 4 July 1985, shortly before the station was closed. As part of this area of London's regeneration, the station reopened in May 2016.

An oddity seen in Perth Station on 9 April 1986 is Class 25 BR/Sulzer type 2 Bo-Bo 97261, previously 25305, and named 'Ethel 2'. The name stood for 'Electric Train Heating Ex-Locomotive', and this was one of three such conversions done in 1983 to provide mobile heating units for trains whose locomotives could not do so. The loco was originally D7655, new in 1966, and was withdrawn from heating duties in 1990.

English Electric type 3 Co-Co 37421 is also at Perth on 9 April 1986, bearing a very striking variation of British Rail corporate livery often associated with Stratford-based locomotives – it was in fact based there at this time, so was very far from home! Originally D6967, it is now preserved.

At Perth too is 350hp 0-6-0 shunter 08882, which appears to be missing its connecting rods. First introduced in 1953, more than a thousand of these locomotives were built over the ensuing nine years, making them the most numerous type of diesel on the BR system. Many remain in use today. This one was new as D4096 in 1961, and spent its entire career in Scotland, until withdrawn in 2005.

In standard BR blue and grey livery, but with Scotrail branding, three-car DMU 101 343 calls at Perth. Metro-Cammell motor brake second SC51795 is nearest the camera.

English Electric type 1 Bo-Bo 20205 is at Perth too on 9 April 1986. New in 1967 as D8305, it is one of 228 of this type built between 1957 and 1968, and is now preserved to main line running standard by the Class 20 Preservation Society.

BRCW type 2 Bo-Bo 27065, accompanying 37421 seen earlier, will be withdrawn three weeks after this picture was taken. New as D5411 to Cricklewood MPD in 1962, in common with all the others on the LMR, it was transferred to Scotland later in the 1960s, concentrating the whole class there. The last of them was withdrawn in 1987.

Arriving at Perth, Brush 4 Co-Co 47704 *Dunedin* bears Scotrail livery, as do some of the carriages it is hauling.

In the same Scotrail livery, fellow Brush type 4 Co-Co 47709 *The Lord Provost* is seen at Edinburgh, Waverley Station on one of the push-pull workings to and from Glasgow, also on 9 April 1986.

On 11 May 1986, six-car Hastings DEMU 1032 heads the Hastings DEMU Farewell Tour at London Underground's Wembley Park Station. As well as touring the various Metropolitan Line branches, it also ventured onto the Stanmore branch of the Jubilee Line, which had originally been part of the Metropolitan Railway and then later part of the Bakerloo Line.

At a very dilapidated Dalston Junction Station, three-car EMU 313008 works the penultimate train to Broad Street on the evening of 27 June 1986. The section of the former North London Line from Dalston West Junction to Broad Street was then closed and, typifying the Thatcher regime's attitude to public transport, the terminus demolished to make way for City office blocks. Fortunately, the path of the railway between Dalston and Shoreditch remained intact, and largely thanks to the Mayor of London, Ken Livingstone, brought back into use and linked with the former East London Line of the London Underground at Shoreditch, forming an integral part of the new London Overground system. Sadly, by the time the line reopened in 2010, his successor, Boris Johnson was Mayor, and took most of the credit for it! Today, a splendid new station stands at Dalston Junction, along with two others, Haggerston and Hoxton, on the line towards Shoreditch which has a frequent service of modern EMUs running from Highbury & Islington to various destinations in south London on London Overground's hugely successful system. What a difference from the rot and decay of the Thatcher years that this picture epitomises!

On 20 July 1986, a four-car BR Derby-built DMU passes through Wendover on a Sunday service from Amersham to Aylesbury on the former Great Central main line. This had been closed north of Aylesbury some twenty years earlier, and at this period its London terminus at Marylebone was threatened with closure, too. Happily, it never happened after all, and today that station is a thriving one!

A peculiar sight at Shanklin Station on 31 July 1986 is that of this former London Underground Standard Stock driving motor car, which has been withdrawn from service on the Ilse of Wight, removed from its bogies, and converted into a store shed!

At Ryde, St. John's Road Depot on the same day is BR 204hp 0-6-0 shunter 03079, the only diesel locomotive on the Isle of Wight. Cars of former London Underground Standard Stock are seen behind it.

An exhibition of railway rolling stock, old and new, was held at Cannon Street Station (then closed at weekends) on 23 and 24 August 1986.
On 23 August 1986, BR Doncaster-built Co-Co 58001 displays its Railfreight livery. It was the first of this class of fifty heavy freight locos
to be built, late in 1982, and although construction continued until 1987, all were withdrawn by 2002. Some, however, saw further use on
the Continent.

Another heavy freight locomotive displayed at Cannon Street that weekend is 56047, one of 135 such engines built between 1976 and 1984. Somewhat curiously, the first thirty were built in Romania, the remainder at BR's Doncaster and Crewe Works. As may be seen, the body shell is similar in appearance to Class 47 locos. Today, few Class 56s remain in service.

At Oxted Station on 13 September 1986, Southern Region four-car DEMU 205016 is part of an eight-car formation that is about to be divided, with the leading unit continuing to East Grinstead and the trailing one to Uckfield. This practice ceased when the line to East Grinstead was electrified in 1987. This unit is one of those originally operated in Hampshire, and in common with the Hastings DEMUs, has its engine compartment behind the driver's cab.

Seen at the original Uckfield Station the same day, four-car unit 207006 is one of the fleet of DEMUs built at Eastleigh for the Oxted line services in 1962. They remained in use on this branch until 2004. The line from Uckfield to Lewes was closed in 1969, and in recent years the terminus at Uckfield has been moved to the east side of the High Street, thus obviating the need for the level crossing seen here. Various plans to reopen the line to Lewes remain unfulfilled.

On 8 November 1986, EMU 312709 is seen at Kings Cross bearing a special headboard proclaiming the extension of electric services on the Great Northern Main Line as far as Huntingdon. Built between 1975 and 1978, these units were the last 'slam-door' multiple units built in Britain, and all were withdrawn by 2004, therefore having much shorter lives than usual for electric rolling stock. This one was built for Great Northern outer suburban use. In retrospect, it seems ridiculous that slam-door units were still being produced as late as 1978.

Brush 2 A1A-A1A 31120, in Railfreight livery, shunts wagons alongside the West Coast Main Line at Carnforth on 17 April 1987.

Also at Carnforth on 17 April 1987, Metro-Cammell motor brake second 54247 heads a two-car unit on a stopping service to Lancaster. In common with a number of DMUs at this period, it has been repainted in 'original' heritage livery – apart from the yellow panel beneath the driver's cab, of course!

Next day, 18 April 1987, I was back in Glasgow, at the Queen Street terminus, where push-pull Brush 4 Co-Co 47707 *Holyrood* awaits departure with a Scotrail service to Edinburgh, with the driving trailer of a push-pull set on the same line in the adjacent platform.

Four loco-hauled passenger services are visible in this view looking down on Glasgow, Queen Street on 20 April 1987. Three Class 47s are seen, along with English Electric type 3 Co-Co 37425 departing on the right. Two DMUs are also just visible.

I travelled homewards from Glasgow via the Settle & Carlisle Line, which at this period was threatened with closure by the Thatcher regime, though fortunately her transport minister Michael Portillo was largely responsible for saving it. I broke my journey at Long Preston, having a pleasant drink in the Boar's Head pub before continuing my journey aboard this BRCW three-car DMU led by car E51830, seen arriving there on 21 April 1987.

The unit seen in the previous picture took me to Skipton, where two-car Pacer unit 142077 is seen when almost new, bearing BR's Provincial Services two-tone blue livery. These dreadful contraptions were based on the design of Leyland National buses. At the time of writing, they are due to be withdrawn by 2019, some possibly replaced by ex-London Underground District Line D Stock EMU cars converted to DEMUs!

A traditional two-car DMU, led by BR Derby motor brake second E53035, arrives at Skipton on the same occasion. This was one of BR's earliest DMUs.

Great Eastern four-car EMU 315854, seen at Broxbourne Station on 2 May 1987, contrasts with former London Transport and London Country RT3461, giving rides in conjunction with the Hoddesdon Model Railway Exhibition that day.

At Liverpool Street Station, Metro-Cammell motor brake second E54041 heads a two-car DMU that has been converted to carry parcels when seen loading up on 12 June 1987.

On 1 August 1987, an unidentified BRCW/Crompton type 3 Bo-Bo shares Portsmouth Harbour terminus was a 4VEP EMU adorned in Network SouthEast livery.

Next day, 2 August 1987, Great Eastern 4-car EMU 315824 departs from Stratford on a local service from Gidea Park to Liverpool Street. At the time of writing, this service (from Shenfield) is still operated by these units, now under the wing of T*f*L Rail, pending its takeover by Crossrail in 2018. On the left, the bay platform in this picture has recently been adapted for the new Docklands Light Railway – there is 'No Service Today' as it did not open until the end of August 1987!

Back on the Southern Region, BRCW/Crompton type 3 Bo-Bo 33008 *Eastleigh* has been restored to 1960s livery, and is seen attached to a 4TC set at Waterloo on 15 August 1987.

On the same day, Hampshire DEMU 205027 arrives at Southampton Central Station. Just visible on the left are this station's nameboards with Network SouthEast branding.

A triumph for Network SouthEast, and indeed one of the very few highlights for British Rail during the Thatcher years, was the reopening of London's Snow Hill Tunnel between Farringdon and Blackfriars Stations, for the introduction of the cross-London Thameslink service. On its first day, 16 May 1988, new four-car EMU 319017 leaves the tunnel and is about to enter Farringdon Station on its way to Bedford. The notice on the wall on the right proclaims the new service; the track in the foreground is the down road from Moorgate. As mentioned earlier, this link had to be removed in order to extend Farringdon Station to this location in order to provide sufficient platform length for longer trains.

The Network SouthEast 'empire' also included the Isle of Wight, where unit 486031 is seen working the Ryde Pier Head to Ryde Esplanade shuttle on 23 July 1988, where it has just disgorged dozens of holidaymakers, including myself and my wife and daughters seen on the left. This unit was unusual in that it made use of the ex-London Transport control trailer, rather than only driving motor cars in the other surviving Standard Stock units. It may well have operated off-peak two-car shuttle services under my home in Canonbury Avenue on the Northern City Line, where such cars were last used by LT until their withdrawal in 1966!

For a time, 4CEP EMUs used on the Hastings main line were painted in this special livery of chocolate brown and grey, with an orange waistband, earning the nickname of 'Jaffa Cakes'. Unit 1565, complete with disgusting graffiti almost blotting out the Network SouthEast logo on its cab, heads a down express at London Bridge on 17 August 1988.

An unusual pairing on a westbound freight train seen heading through Camden Road Station on 20 April 1989 is English Electric type 3 Co-Co 37158 and a Class 56 diesel.

Further along the North London Line that day, Bulleid-designed 2EPB EMU 6331 approaches Hampstead Heath Station on a North Woolwich to Richmond working. Again, its cab has been besmirched by graffiti. In the autumn, these units would be replaced by Class 313 three-car sets purloined from my local Great Northern suburban services, and returned to their native Southern Region.

Back on the Isle of Wight, BR 204hp diesel mechanical shunter 03179 is seen newly repainted in Network SouthEast livery at Ryde, St. John's Road depot on 2 August 1989. Somewhat oddly it had replaced classmate 03079 (seen earlier). The latter is now preserved; this one was subsequently transferred to my local Hornsey EMU depot where at the time of writing it remains, but out of use.

Also smartly adorned in NSE livery, Hampshire three-car DEMU 205026 accompanies a 4CIG EMU at Portsmouth Harbour terminus on 5 August 1989.

Adorned in an approximation of GWR livery, Brush 4 Co-Co 47484 *Isambard Kingdom Brunel* arrives at Paddington with an up express in September 1989. Following withdrawal in 1998, this locomotive was preserved.

On the same day, Pressed Steel single unit L122 (motor brake second car 55022) sets off from Greenford on the Greenford Loop shuttle service to Ealing Broadway. The bay platform for this service here is unusual in that it is situated between the two tracks of the London Underground Central Line. Trains for Ealing Broadway dive beneath the westbound Central Line track just south of the station to reach the loop.

At Stratford Low-Level Station on 28 September 1989, Bulleid-designed Southern Region 2EPB units 6318 and 6330 are seen on the North London Line North Woolwich to Richmond service shortly before their replacement by Class 313 EMUs. This part of the station has changed beyond recognition since this picture was taken, and these two platforms are now served by Docklands Light Railway trains running between Stratford International and Beckton or Woolwich Arsenal.

Pressed Steel single unit L125 (motor brake second 55025) is one of two seen at Acton Main Line Station on 14 October 1989 working a through service from Paddington to Greenford via Ealing Broadway. When Crossrail takes over suburban services running from Paddington in 2018, the Greenford loop service will be an anomaly, and will be curtailed at West Ealing rather than continuing to Ealing Broadway. As this book goes to press, it is being suggested that Chiltern Railways will take over this service when Crossrail becomes fully operational.

At Clapham Junction on 20 April 1990, a good variety of rolling stock may be seen, ranging from an English Electric Class 50 Co-Co diesel to a Class 73 electro-diesel Bo-Bo and various types of Southern Region EMUs. Everything is in Network SouthEast livery, except for the Class 73 which still carries Inter City colours, since it is used on the Gatwick Express service.

In May 1990, Bulleid Southern Region 4EPB unit 5121 is at the trailing end of an eight-car formation leaving Lewisham Station for Charing Cross. The leading unit, in NSE livery, is about to pass beneath the bridge at St. John's which collapsed upon being struck by wreckage from the disastrous collision there in December 1957.

Seen at Kings Cross in June 1990, English Electric 350hp 0-6-0 shunter 08834 is very smartly turned out when in use as station pilot. Dating from 1960, it remains in use at the time of writing. On the far right, the overgrown remains of the platform of York Way Station may be seen.

On the same occasion, HST unit 43119 leaves Kings Cross for the North, shortly after many of these units were displaced by the electrification of the Great Northern main line.

At Sandown Station in July 1990, ex-LT Standard Stock unit 485043 is the last of the type still in service on the Isle of Wight, and contrasts with 'new' 1938 Stock unit 003. It is hard to believe that some of the antiquated-looking Standard Stock cars were built as late as 1934, just four years before the 1938 Stock, which still looks modern today!

Rebuilding work is going on at Liverpool Street Station in August 1990, as English Electric type 3 Co-Co 37140 and a Class 86 Bo-Bo electric locomotive occupy the tracks which once connected here with the Metropolitan Railway and, in doing so, effectively cut the original station concourse in half.

On 20 September 1990 at Upper Holloway station, Pressed Steel single unit L125 (driving brake motor 55025) still carries Thames logos for its original home on suburban services out of Paddington, as seen earlier, but has been pressed into service on the Barking to Gospel Oak Line. Eastbound rush hour passengers struggle to board the already overcrowded car, as seen here.

Also in September 1990, Great Eastern suburban unit 305407 at the trailing end of a six-car formation of two of these units departing from Seven Sisters Station. Built originally in 1959/60 for the electrification of local services between Liverpool Street and Cheshunt, Chingford or Enfield Town, these units were now on their way out, though some saw further service in the Manchester area.

Different liveries are borne by two English Electric type 3 Co-Cos, seen propelling a container freight off the North London Line onto the Great Eastern Main Line at Stratford, also in September 1990.

On the same day, three-car EMU 305403 was towed by English Electric type 3 Co-Co 37140 on a special service to and from Stratford via South Tottenham and Seven Sisters in connection with a Network SouthEast Gala Day at Enfield Town Station, where it is seen here. Note the headboard showing the name 'West Anglia', later adopted for services running from Liverpool Street to Cambridge, Hertford East, Cheshunt, Chingford and Enfield Town. Inner suburban services to the latter three destinations were taken over by London Overground in May 2015.

New four-car EMU 321432 is seen at a wet and dismal Watford North Station on New Year's Day 1991, working the shuttle service between Watford Junction and St. Albans Abbey. This type of EMU seems rather extravagant for such a backwater as this!

On a cold, crisp January day in 1991, three-car EMU 305401, another in NSE livery, heads a six-car local service to Liverpool Street into Silver Street Station, Edmonton.

At a display of rolling stock in the Brighton side of London Bridge Station in March 1991, new Canadian-built General Motors Co-Co 59104 bears the livery of its owner, Amey Roadstone Construction.

BR Ashford-built 2EPB units 6223, 6244 and 6213 are seen outside Slade Green EMU depot on the same day. Along with the earlier Bulleid-designed 4EPBs, such units were the mainstay of North Kent Line and Dartford Loop services, now branded 'Kent Link', for more than forty years.

Earlier Bulleid S.R. 4SUB unit 4732, now preserved in an approximation of its original green livery, is seen departing London Underground's District Line Wimbledon Park Station in conjunction with an open-day at the nearby NSE Durnsford Road Depot in May 1991.

A variety of diesel and electric rolling stock was on display at the depot itself. EMU 016 is an NSE departmental unit formed of former 4SUB stock, used as a rail cleaning unit, to rid tracks and especially conductor rails of leaves, ice or snow. It contrasts with the new Class 319 unit on the right.

One of the units built in 1960 for the London, Tilbury & Southend line electrification, but initially used on local services out of Liverpool Street, four car EMU 302223 has recently been refurbished and painted in NSE livery when seen in August 1991 passing Shadwell DLR Station on its way to Shoeburyness.

Class 50 English Electric Co-Cos were now being retired from their duties hauling expresses from Waterloo to Exeter, but 50033 *Glorious* seems in fine form when speeding through Clapham Junction, also in August 1991, with a down express. After withdrawal in 1994 it was preserved.

Seen at an open day at Old Oak Common MPD in August 1991, Clayton type 1 Bo-Bo D8568 represents one of the shortest-lived classes of diesel locomotive on the British Rail system. New only in 1964, it was withdrawn in 1971 but later secured for preservation. These locomotives were generally based in Scotland and the North East of England during their short lives. Built between 1962 and 1965, all were withdrawn by the end of 1971.

More at home at Old Oak Common are three of the diesel hydraulic types that dominated the Great Western main lines during the 1960's – Hymek D7018, Warship D821 *Greyhound* and Western D1015 *Western Champion*. All are smartly preserved in liveries they would have carried in those years. A recent Class 59 diesel accompanies them on the extreme right.

On a fine summer's evening in the same month, refurbished 4CEP unit 1557 arrives at Chestfield & Swalecliffe Halt with an up express from Ramsgate to Victoria. I have many happy memories of travelling on these units when they were new, to and from family holidays here between 1959 and 1965, and rode homewards on this one.

In contrast to former Western Region three-car DMUs also used on this service at this period, BR Eastleigh-built three-car DEMU 205029, originally one of the Hampshire units, is seen working the evening rush hour service from Clapham Junction to Kensington, Olympia. In this view, the driving motor car is at the trailing end.

At Clapham Junction, the same day, also in August 1991, Royal Mail-liveried Brush 4 47703 *The Queen Mother* is seen in the sidings attached to a set of NSE Mk2 carriages, presumably having worked an Exeter-Waterloo express.

More mundane is NSE-liveried Bulleid 2EPB unit 6305, at the trailing end of a stopping service which has just departed from Battersea Park Station for Victoria. It is back on former Southern Region metals, having worked on the North London Line between 1985 and 1989.

Perhaps illustrating one of the perceived dangers slam-door rolling stock, passengers on LT&S four-car EMU 302203 already have some of its doors open as it arrives at Benfleet Station on August Bank Holiday Monday 1991.

Seen outside Marylebone Station in March 1992 are a number of first-generation BR Derby-built DMU cars, now being withdrawn as a result of replacement by new Class 165 Turbo DMUs.

At Gunnersbury Station in June 1992, three car EMU 313003 has for some reason been terminated short of Richmond as its 'tipped out' passengers wait to continue their journey whilst it is reversed to return to North Woolwich. The North London Line was gaining a reputation for unreliability at this time, and this got much worse after privatisation. At least the frustrated passengers had the additional option of the District Line to continue their journeys from here!

At Liverpool Street on 28 June 1992, former LT&S EMU 302990 is seen in use for Royal Mail postal transport in the company of a Class 86 electric loco which has arrived from Norwich.

Hybrid West Anglia four-car EMU 302596 has been besmirched by this disgusting graffiti when seen working a Chingford to Liverpool Street service at Hackney Downs in May 1993. By now, these units too were on their way out.

On 29 May 1993, the end has come for the 1940 Bulleid-designed Waterloo &City Line tube cars. Following the building of the Eurostar terminus at Waterloo, the lift that used to be their means of access to the surface was removed, therefore they had to be lifted out by crane from their depot at the end of their platforms at Waterloo. Here, a double-ended driving motor car is hoisted high above Lower Marsh prior to being taken away by low-loader.

For an open day at the Quainton Railway Centre on 31 May 1993, new Chiltern Lines two-car Turbo unit 165028 is working a special 'Quainton Turbo' to and from Aylesbury on the former Great Central Main Line. What a scandal that this main line was closed almost two years after Harold Wilson's Labour government – which had campaigned on the basis of halting the railway closures of the notorious 'Beeching Plan' – came to power!

Seen at Gatwick Airport Station on 18 July 1993, electro-diesel Bo-Bo 73202 *Royal Observer Corps* heads one of the Gatwick Express push-pull units. Of interest is the '73A' (Stewarts Lane) shedplate on the front.

Early Brush 2 A1A-A1A 31107 *John H Carless VC* is seen at Old Oak Common MPD on 26 March 1994. This had been new to the Eastern Region as D5525 in 1959.

BR 350hp 0-6-0 diesel shunter 08948 is one of two immaculately turned out and attached to a snowplough, also on show at Old Oak Common that day.

At Olympia on 28 May 1994, a former Western Region two-car Pressed Steel DMU is seen on the Willesden Junction to Clapham Junction North London Line service which has just been introduced and is advertised by a banner on the station footbridge. This was electrified, using class 313 EMUs, two years later. The two third-rail electrified tracks in the foreground are for Eurostar Channel Tunnel units running to and from their depot at Old Oak Common. Note also the newly-built platform for the new NLR service – at this period, the North Woolwich to Stratford, Barking to Gospel Oak and Euston to Watford DC lines, along with this one, were being branded 'North London Railways'.

In June 1994, Mendip Rail Yeoman Co-Co 59005 *Kenneth J Painter* hauls a long line of aggregate wagons through Highbury & Islington Station on the North London Line, in the capable hands of driver Keith Grimes. These locos, built by General Motors, were the first United States-built ones to be used on the British main line railway system, and were the forerunners of the numerous Class 66 locomotives in service today.

At Rye Station in July 1994, two Oxted Line DEMU's pass on the Ashford to Hastings 'Marshlink' service. Both have been reduced to two-car units by the removal of their original centre trailer car. Unit 207202 bound for Hastings is in the foreground.

At Hastings Station on the same day, 4CEP unit 1516 heads an eight-car formation bound for Charing Cross. Such units were some of the last former Southern Region 'slam-door' EMUs to be withdrawn some ten years after this picture was taken.

One of the later 4CIG EMUs, 1884, is seen at Lymington Pier on the shuttle service to and from Brockenhurst in August 1994. This branch was home to the very last 'slam-door' EMUs in 2010, having retained them for five years after their withdrawal on the rest of the former Southern Region network.

Representing a new generation of British-built diesel locomotives, Brush Co-Co 60037 stands at Reading General Station bearing Transrail livery on 18 March 1995.

A stranger at London Underground's Watford Metropolitan Line Station on 20 May 1995 is former Hampshire Lines BR Eastleigh-built three-car DEMU 205009. It is laying over between trips from there to and from Chesham, in connection with LU's annual 'Steam on the Met' event, and was usually in service from London Bridge or Victoria to Uckfield at the time.

While the North London Line was being converted to 25kv overhead electrification between Camden Road and Willesden Junction in the autumn of 1996, services between Willesden Junction High Level and Gunnersbury (where passengers for Kew Gardens and Richmond had to change to LU District Line trains) were provided by DMUs usually used on North London Railways' Barking to Gospel Oak and Willesden Junction to Clapham Junction services. Pressed Steel two-car DMU L700 is seen calling at South Acton Station on the way back to Willesden. The space behind the station buildings on the left is where trains on the District Line shuttle service to and from Acton Town once terminated. Today, a block of flats occupies the site.

About the Author

I was born at the end of 1947, just five days before the 'Big Four' railway companies, and many bus companies – including London Transport – were nationalised by Clement Attlee's Labour government.

Like most young lads born in the early post-war years, I soon developed a passionate interest in railways, the myriad steam engines still running on Britain's railways in those days in particular. However, because my home in Canonbury Avenue, Islington was just a few minutes' walk from North London's last two tram routes, the 33 in Essex Road and the 35 in Holloway Road and Upper Street, my parents often took me on these for outings to the South Bank, particularly to the Festival of Britain which was held there in the last summer they ran, in 1951. Moreover, my father worked at the GPO's West Central District Office in Holborn and often travelled to and from work on the 35 tram. As a result, he knew many of the tram crews, who would let me stand by the driver at the front of the trams as they travelled through the Kingsway Tram Subway. This was an unforgettable experience for a four-year-old! In addition, my home was in the heart of North London's trolleybus system, with route 611 actually passing the door, and one of the busiest and complicated trolleybus junctions in the world, at Holloway, Nag's Head, a short ride away along Holloway Road. Here, the trolleybuses' overhead almost blotted out the sky! Thus, from a very early age, I developed an equal interest in buses and trolleybuses to that in railways, and have retained both until the present day.

I was educated at my local Highbury County Grammar School, and later at Kingsway College, by coincidence a stone's throw from the old tram subway. I was first bought a camera for my fourteenth birthday at the end of 1961, which was immediately put to good use photographing the last London trolleybuses in North West London on their very snowy last day a week later. Three years later, I started work as an administrator for the old London County Council at County Hall, by coincidence adjacent to the former Festival of Britain site, and travelled to and from work on bus routes 171 or 172, which had replaced the 33 and 35 trams mentioned above.

By now, my interest in buses and trolleybuses had expanded to include those of other operators, and I travelled throughout England and Wales between 1961 and 1968 in pursuit of them, being able to afford to travel further afield after starting work! I also bought a colour cine-camera in 1965, with which I was able to capture what is now very rare footage of long-lost buses, trolleybuses and steam locomotives. Where the latter are concerned, I was one of the initial purchasers of the unique British Railways 'Pacific' locomotive 71000 *Duke of Gloucester*, which was the last ever passenger express engine built for use in Britain. Other preservationists laughed at the group which purchased what in effect was a cannibalised hulk from Barry scrapyard at the end of 1973, but they laughed on the other side of their faces when, after extensive and innovative rebuilding, it steamed again in 1986. It has since become one of the best-known and loved preserved British locomotives, often returning to the main lines.

Although I spent 35 years in local government administration, with the LCC's successor, the Greater London Council, then Haringey Council and finally literally back on my old doorstep, with Islington Council, I also took a break from office drudgery in 1974/75 and actually worked on the buses as a conductor at London Transport's Clapton Garage, on local routes 22, 38 and 253. Working on the latter, a former tram and trolleybus route, in particular was an unforgettable experience! I was recommended for promotion as an inspector, but rightly thought that taking such a job with the surname Blake was unwise in view of the then-current character of the same name and occupation in the 'On The Buses' TV series and films, and so declined the offer and returned to County Hall!

By this time, I had begun to have my transport photographs published in various books and magazines featuring buses and railways, and also started off the North London Transport Society, which catered for enthusiasts interested in both subjects. In conjunction with this group, I have also compiled and published a number of books on the subject since 1977, featuring many of the 100,000 or so transport photographs I have taken over the years.

Also through the North London Transport Society, I became involved in setting up and organising various events for transport enthusiasts in 1980, notably the North Weald Bus Rally which the group took over in 1984. **This raised thousands of pounds for charity until its discontinuation in 2016. Many of the other events are still going strong today**.

In addition to my interest in public transport, I also have an interest in the popular music of the late 1950s and early 1960s, in particular that of the eccentric independent record producer, songwriter and manager Joe Meek, in whose tiny studio above a shop in Holloway Road (not far from the famous trolleybus junction) he wrote and produced *Telstar* by The Tornados, which became the first British pop record to make No.1 in America, at the end of 1962, long before The Beatles had even been heard of over there! When Joe died in February 1967, I set up an Appreciation Society for his music, which has a very distinctive sound. That society is also still going strong today, too.

I also enjoy a pint or two (and usually more) of real ale, and I have two grown-up daughters, Margaret and Felicity, and three grandchildren, Gracie, Freddie and Oscar, at the time of writing. I still live in North London, having moved to my present home in Palmers Green in 1982.

31 1723

WHAT HAPPENS WHEN

my sibling has cancer

written + illustrated by
SARA OLSHER

Hi, my name is Mia!

And this is Stuart.
Stuart feels better when he knows
what's going to happen every day.

(Actually, *everybody* feels better when they know
what's going to happen—even grown-ups!)

Most of the time,
we do the same things in the mornings.
We wake up.

We eat breakfast.
(I like apples. Stuart only eats bugs.)

Usually our nights are the same too.
We brush our teeth.

We put on our jammies, and we go to bed.
Every day ends with sleep.

But our days can be different.

Some days we go to school,
and some days are the weekend!

When something big changes,
what we do each day can change too.
Stuart wants to know what happens to our days
when our brother or sister has **cancer**.

But he doesn't really understand what cancer is. Do you?
Cancer is sort of like a sickness,
but you can't catch it like you catch a cold.

Here's how it works!

Every living thing is made up of tiny little guys called **cells**.

Cells are like blocks, but they put *themselves* together.
One really cool thing about cells is that one cell can
turn itself into two cells anytime it wants.
(*Whoa*, right?)

That means cells can build and build and build.
It's like building with LEGO™ and *never* running out of blocks!

imagine the tower you could build!

Every cell has a job.
Together they build body parts, then tell them how to work.
They make hearts pump, legs walk, lungs breathe,
and so much more!

Cells are very polite.
They give each other space to work,
and they stop making new cells when they have enough to do a job.

But sometimes a broken cell gets made.
It looks weird, acts weird, and doesn't know what its job is.
The only thing it remembers how to do is make more cells.

Nobody caused this cell to break.
It wasn't anything the person ate or did wrong! Sometimes cells break.

And one or two broken cells is no big deal,
because our healthy cells can get rid of them.
But sometimes the healthy cells don't see the broken cells ...

... and the broken cells keep making
more and more broken cells, faster and faster.

Before long, it's a *huge* mess.
This huge mess of broken cells is called cancer.

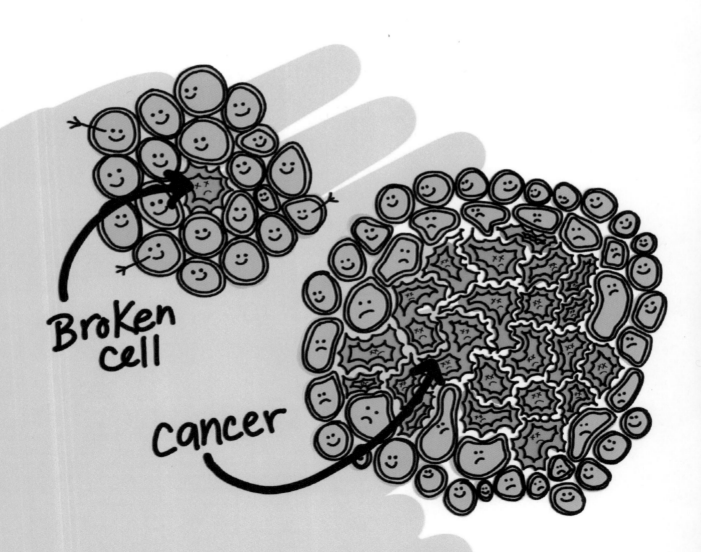

Broken
cell

cancer

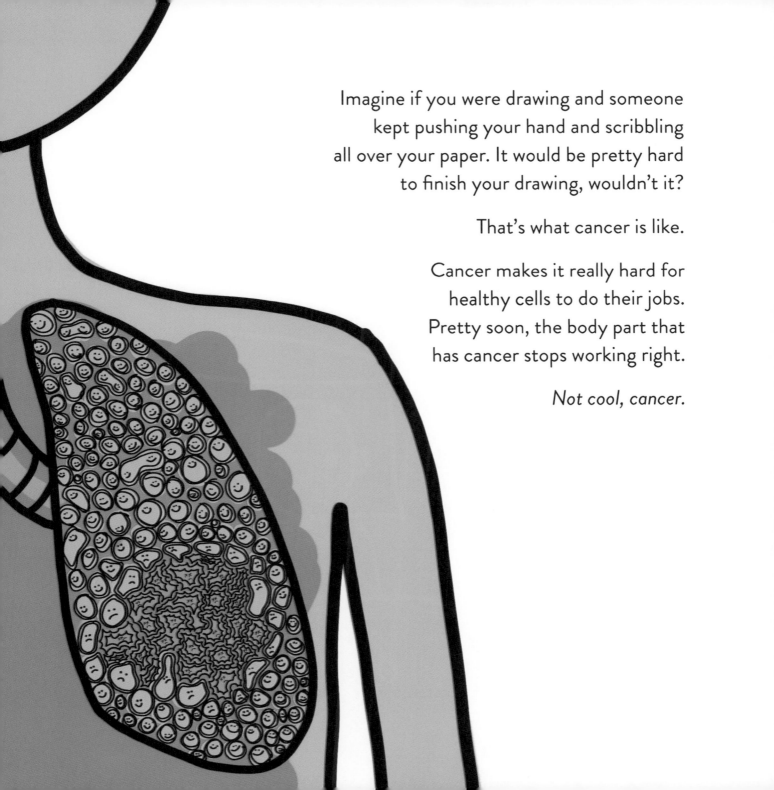

Imagine if you were drawing and someone kept pushing your hand and scribbling all over your paper. It would be pretty hard to finish your drawing, wouldn't it?

That's what cancer is like.

Cancer makes it really hard for healthy cells to do their jobs. Pretty soon, the body part that has cancer stops working right.

Not cool, cancer.

When our healthy cells get crowded by cancer,
they aren't able to do their jobs.
And if they can't do their jobs, our bodies might not work right.

So when someone finds cancer in their body,
they definitely want to get it out.

To get the cancer out, sometimes a
doctor will give someone surgery.

This means the doctors will make the
person go to sleep at the hospital, then
carefully take out the broken cells.
The person doesn't feel anything.

This might mean the person isn't home for a
few days, because they are at the hospital.

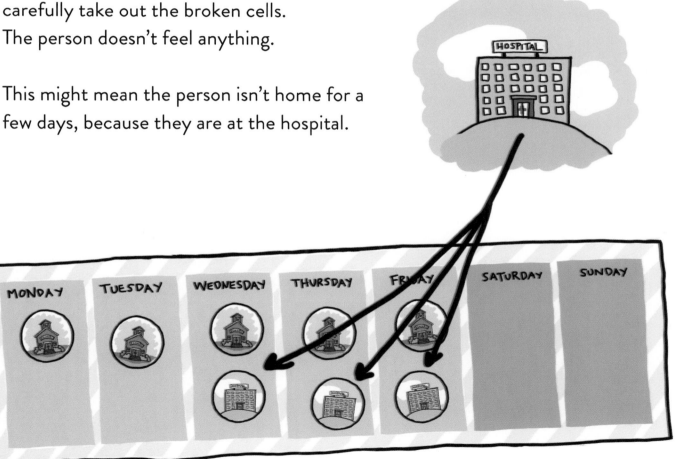

Doctors can also give the person medicine called chemo or chemotherapy. The chemo medicine gets rid of the cancer, but it also does some very not-fun things.

One thing it does is kind of weird and maybe funny and also sad: It can make the person's hair fall out, so they are totally bald until they are done with chemo.

It also makes the person feel tired or sick for a long time. They can't run, jump, or play like they're used to.

Sometimes, the doctors use a big machine to zap the cancer cells with a heat ray called radiation, and they all go away.

To get radiation, the person lays on a table while a machine sends out the rays. The person will go to the doctor for radiation every day (except the weekends) for many weeks.

Radiation doesn't hurt, but the person's skin might turn red, like a sunburn, and they also might get tired.

Both of these things go away pretty quickly after radiation is over.

Oh well, it won't last forever...

To get chemo, the person goes to a doctor appointment and sits in a chair for a few hours while medicine goes in their body.

Sometimes they go every week, and sometimes they go every few weeks. Sometimes they might stay overnight at the hospital. A grown-up will go with them.

Either way, they usually get chemo for months.

All this makes Stuart a little nervous.
He wants to know - what about me?
What's going to happen?

If your sibling gets the chemo medicine, there are some days where it doesn't bother them very much. You can play quiet games or do a craft together. Or, they might still feel like running and playing! There are a lot of activitites to look forward to.

But other days, your brother or sister's body might hurt or feel tired.
On those days, they might need to do quiet activities,
like watch a movie — or they might just need to sleep.

Sometimes this is scary. You are used to seeing them
strong and active! Chemo makes their body feel weak, but they are still the
same person — and inside they are still strong. They're just tired.

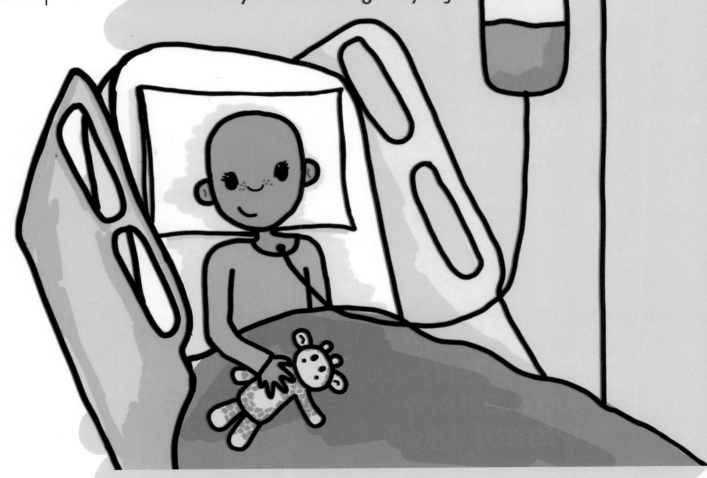

When a brother or sister gets cancer, everyone in the family has very big feelings. It might mean that your parents are sad and cry sometimes, or they get mad easier than they used to.

Lots of things are different after cancer, like:

Your parents might be extra busy with doctor appointments or trips to the hospital.

Your house might feel extra NOISY or Quiet

because people are there to help!

because your sibling is sleeping or at the hospital.

maybe your sibling is acting different because they are tired or having BIG feelings.

maybe you are acting different too!

Your family might be extra careful about germs. People with cancer can get sick easily.

BIG changes like these can make you feel lonely.

Feeling lonely is normal. You might feel *lots* of big feelings.
You might feel jealous of your brother or sister for getting more attention.
Then you might feel bad for feeling that way. You might feel scared
or angry or sad or confused. All of these feelings are okay.

It's okay to be happy, too. It's okay to laugh, even when things are hard.

You know what else is okay? Missing how things used to be!
It won't be this way forever, and there are lots of ways to feel better, like:

Unfortunately, there's nothing you can do to make cancer go away yourself.
You didn't make it happen (that's impossible), and you can't stop it either.

That is frustrating. But there *are* some ways to help your
brother or sister, like reading a book to them, making them laugh,
playing a game, listening to music, or getting them a snack.

Some people have a cancer that will go away forever. Some people have cancer that goes away for awhile and then comes back.

All the changes that come with cancer definitely aren't fun, but when you know what to expect, they aren't scary either.

And there are lots of things to celebrate!
Your family is learning to do hard things together.

Every time your brother or sister finishes chemo or radiation or comes
home from the hospital, your family should definitely celebrate!

And of course, if cancer goes away, all the cells are doing their jobs,
and the body is healthy again. And you know what that means?
A healthy body that can run, jump,
swim and play again . . . and grow new hair!

Stuart feels a lot better now that he knows what to expect.
Even though our days can be different, it helps to plan out our
week together so we know what's going to happen next.

We can give ourselves activities to look forward to, like making crafts,
watching a movie, or going to a friend's house to play.

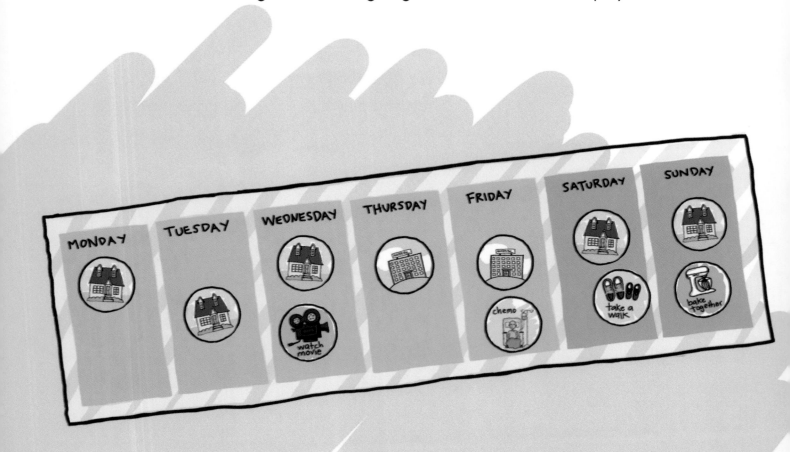

And remember, your family loves you so much. You are a very important person to them! It's important to share your worries and feelings with a grown-up. All these changes can be hard!

By planning special time together, you have a time when you know it's okay to talk about your feelings. *We can do hard things, together!*

And don't forget, Stuart... even the biggest feelings don't last forever.

Hi! My name is Sara, and I had cancer, too.

I wrote this book (and 6 others!) because I like to draw + help people.

Things I LOVE!

- reading
- Dancing (Badly)
- my family
- nature
- animals
- candy
- Rainbows
- Quiet time

(for awhile I didn't have any hair. I think my head is a lovely shape.)

I live with my daughter and our cats, Tater, Waffle + Batman. One day, I want a goat, and I want to name him CAULIFLOWER!

 I do all my drawings on an iPad with an Apple pencil

Hey Parents!

Let's be real: literally nobody wants to tell their kids they have cancer.

As a cancer survivor myself, I've been there.

Get this PDF guide for free with the coupon **BOOKDEAL**

Mighty + Bright's psychologist-approved guide for talking to kids will help reduce stress and anxiety for the whole family.

You'll learn:
- How to tell kids about your diagnosis;
- How to encourage open communication;
- Applies to all types of cancers and all types of people (parents, siblings, grandparents, friends);
- Digital copy, so you can use it, like, right now.

SCAN THIS USING YOUR PHONE
or visit: mightyandbright.com/cancer-guide

mighty + bright™

Published by Mighty + Bright
mightyandbright.com

ISBN: 979-8-9851984-0-9

Want to tell me something?
Send a letter!
mia
c/o mighty + bright
555 5th Street #300F
Santa Rosa CA 95401